D-I-S-C-I-P-L-E

D-I-S-C-I-P-L-E

Eight Essential Elements To Foster Christlikeness

Dr. Alice T. O'Neal

XULON PRESS

Xulon Press Elite
2301 Lucien Way #415
Maitland, FL 32751
407.339.4217
www.xulonpress.com

Unless otherwise indicated, Scripture quotations taken from the King James Version (KJV) – *public domain.*

Paperback ISBN-13: 978-1-66286-388-2
Hard Cover ISBN-13: 978-1-66286-389-9
Ebook ISBN-13: 978-1-66286-390-5

TABLE OF CONTENTS

STATEMENTS OF ENDORSEMENT

Dr. Alice T. O'Neal's <u>D-I-S-C-I-P-L-E: Eight Essential Elements to Foster Christlikeness</u> provides churches and leaders with an excellent resource for discipleship. Far too many Christians never grow because they have never fostered good solid spiritual disciplines such as prayer, stewardship, fellowship in a small group, tithing, daily Bible reading, and fasting.

Dr. O'Neal has provided a way to foster Christlikeness by providing eight essential training segments that develop solid spiritual habits and character. Being a Christian is about living a life that embodies who Christ was while on Earth and still is today. This book allows you to advance through the stages of discipleship and pattern your daily habits after the life of Christ.

I wholeheartedly recommend <u>D-I-S-C-I-P-L-E: Eight Essential Elements to Foster Christlikeness</u> for our spiritual growth and focus on discipleship. This book is a welcomed aid for pastors and leaders alike. The church today needs leaders and shepherds who understand the actual call of Christian discipleship and have the ability to teach and instruct God's people.

Apostle Charles E. Lewis, Sr. D.MIN
Senior Pastor Antioch & Kairos Church Ministries

<u>D-I-S-C-I-P-L-E: Eight Essential Elements to Foster Christlikeness</u> is a most valuable and essential reading that gives practical and easy to follow directives in developing Christian maturity. Dr. Alice T. O'Neal gives explicit application to follow to achieve these goals. I highly recommend this book to anyone who wishes to develop in Christlike qualities and Christlike maturity. The eight elements given are essential in becoming mature in Christ and living a life wherein Christlikeness can be seen.

Pastor Janet T. Grady
Bay Chapel Free Will Baptist Church

The Scripture text in Romans 8:29 provides the enlightenment that it is God's will for the followers of Christ to become like Him. The term conform in this verse is indicative of the spiritual formation process toward the goal of Christlikeness which is the basic topic of this book. Thus, this confirmation from the Word of God that the subject of this book is in agreement with what God desires and wills for His sons and daughters provides affirmation of this book as a commendable Christian education resource.

CHAPTER 1

INTRODUCTION

E ffective Christian education in the church setting should be a process that stimulates growth. The problem is that without the provision and engagement in the essential elements of Christian education believers can attend church for an entire life span and never grow into Christlike maturity. This book provides a paradigm that can be utilized to foster the demonstration of Christlikeness by individual maturation towards spiritual formation and the operationalizing of the community of believers as a life-giving organism. The content of this book is the outcome of a research approach which included the examination of recognized models of Christian education, spiritual formation, and Christian community development. Additionally, pastors of fifteen churches in eastern North Carolina of each congregational size, mega, large, medium, and small were surveyed regarding the model of Christian education utilized. The full research project reference link is: https://digitalcommons.liberty.edu/doctoral/2360/.

Key terms used in this book include Christian education, Christlikeness, disciple, discipleship, spiritual formation, and Christian community. The context of Christian education relative to this paradigm is provided as a component of the church ministry often referred to interchangeably as a Christian education ministry. Thus, the paradigm of spiritual development in this book which is amenable to individual or small group study forums addresses Christian education that involves the impartation of foundational Christian doctrine and principles. The term Christlikeness may be used synonymously in reference to Christian maturity. Christlikeness encompasses imitating and exhibiting behavioral and verbal actions/responses that are consistent with what Jesus would do if He were (you) the individual in that situation. Disciple and discipleship in this book refer to an individual (disciple) who has made a decision to be a follower of Jesus Christ and is engaged in an ongoing process (discipleship) to learn how to be His follower. Spiritual formation in this work is defined as the process of spiritual change that the follower of Jesus Christ undergoes. This concept of spiritual formation is highly associated with the term transformation and is often used interchangeably. Both terms denote the process of the follower becoming increasingly more like the teacher, Jesus Christ.[1] Last, the Christian community is defined as a group of persons of like faith and purpose with whom the follower is interpersonally connected.

CHAPTER 2

CHRISTIAN EDUCATION: AN ESSENTIAL PROCESS

C hristian education is deemed as an essential process that involves the impartation of foundational Christian doctrine and principles, is consistent with the mandate of the Great Commission. Particularly, this command as delineated by Jesus is to be executed by the church universally in order to make other followers of Jesus Christ and teach them about Him, to believe in Him, and to obey Him (Matt. 28:18-20). Accordingly, Kenneth O. Gangel described that "in its simplest and purest form, Christian education is communicating God's truth in order to make disciples."[2] Thus, Gangel supports the premise of this book that a sincere biblical disciple exhibits the evidence of spiritual growth by hearing, understanding, and obeying the teachings of Christ that reflect the fruit of life changes and help disciples make other disciples.[3] Subsequently, the application of the command of Christ indicates that the growth and development of the believer are concurrently internal, which entails "becoming like Christ in word, thought, and attitude," and external, which encompasses "becoming like Christ in action."[4] Notably, the essential process of Christian education as it relates to spiritual growth relative to the discipleship process was delineated by Eleanor Daniel:

> The purpose of Bible teaching is to bring change into the life of the learner until he has reached maturity in Christ—a lifelong task. This maturity is achieved when a person has a knowledge of God's Word, with understanding, that results in changed behavior: bearing fruit, growing in knowledge, becoming stronger in endurances and patience, and being thankful. [5]

Thus, Christian education provides fundamental instructions to believers to foster the impartation of biblical understanding, essential faith, empowerment, and resources to make quality decisions to live, follow, and pursue the way of Jesus Christ in the midst of the present-day diverse public sector.[6] Therefore, an essential objective of Christian education is attending to how believers form an identity and vocation of being followers of the way of Jesus in their perceptions of themselves and being known by others as a follower of the way of Jesus.[7] Subsequently, the task of Christian education entails the employment of a process that encourages and facilitates individually and corporately the spiritual growth of the life of the body of believers, forming it toward Christlikeness, and empowering it as an effective witness and "communicator of power of the gospel."[8]

CHAPTER 3

FOUNDATIONAL FACTORS
RELATIVE TO SPIRITUAL LIFE

When the culmination of this dispensation of grace transpires, some individuals may experience the comparable reward of hearing the Lord say to him/her, "Well done, thou good and faithful servant … enter thou into the joy of thy Lord" (Matt. 25:21).[9] However, other individuals may experience the repercussion of hearing the Lord say, "I tell you, I know you not whence ye are; depart from me, all ye workers of iniquity" (Luke 13:27). As the gospel of Christ is proclaimed, which is "the power of God to salvation for everyone who believes," each individual will be afforded the opportunity to become a good, faithful servant unto the Lord (Rom. 1:16; Matt. 24:14 NKJV).[10] Thus, an individual's spiritual life as a follower of Jesus commences when he/she is born again according to Scripture as Jesus explicated in John 3:3-7. Subsequent to the individual's spiritual new birth, which is a work of God, volitionally, he/she can engage in the essential process of Christian education, which entails the lifelong progressive transformation to become a mature, faithful, and effective follower of Christ.[11] This newly converted believer who is in infancy stage or stage one of discipleship may choose to begin his/her discipleship process in a

Christian community setting that uses individual one-to-one mentoring/discipling, small group engagement, study groups, spiritual coaching, or other Christian spiritual formation and training settings/forums. Regardless of the forum in which the believer's discipleship process commences, it is recommended for the leader/discipler to assist the individual in examining the foundational factor relative to this new believer's spiritual life by affirming or reaffirming his/her salvation experience through a participatory review of the gospel plan of salvation in accordance with Scripture foundational truth. The process of guiding and reviewing the plan of salvation with the believer allows him/her to have the assurance of salvation based on Scripture and begins to equip the individual with the Scripture to share his/her faith with others. Additionally, having the assurance of salvation by faith based on Scripture understanding and revelation helps to equip the believer to stand firm in his/her convictions when the spiritual, emotional, physical, and social vicissitudes and challenges of life surge, and the enemy accuses him/her of "not being saved" and/or "not being a good Christian."

The following delineation of statements, questions, Scripture, prayer, and declarations is a guide to salvation based on the gospel message that can be used with seekers and new converts at stage one of discipleship engagement:

Guide to Salvation

"God wants you to know..."

1. He loves you and has a plan for you![12]

Read what the Bible says, "For God so loved the world that he gave his only begotten Son, that whosoever believeth in him should not perish, but have everlasting life." (John 3:16)[13]

Jesus said, "I am come that they might have life, and that they might have it more abundantly." (John 10:10)

However, here is the problem:

2. "Mankind is sinful and separated from God."[14]

We have all done, thought, or said bad things that the Bible calls "sin."

Read what the Bible says, "For all have sinned, and come short of the glory of God." (Rom. 3:23)

The result of sin is death, spiritual separation from God.

Now read what the Bible says, "For the wages of sin is death; but the gift of God is eternal life through Jesus Christ our Lord." (Rom. 6:23)

The good news is: "Jesus Christ is God's only provision for mankind's sin."[15]

3. God sent His Son, Jesus, to die for your sins!

Jesus died in our place so we could live with Him in eternity.

Read what the Bible says, "But God commendeth His love toward us, in that, while we were yet sinners, Christ died for us." (Rom. 5:8)

However, it did not end with Christ's death on the cross. He rose again and still lives!

"Christ died for our sins ... He was buried. ... He was raised on the third day according to the Scriptures."[16]

Read what the Bible says, "For I delivered unto you first of all that which I also received, how that Christ died for our sins according to the scriptures; And that he was buried, and that he rose again the third day according to the scriptures." (1 Cor. 15:3-4)

Jesus is the only way to God.

Read what the Bible says, "Jesus saith unto him, I am the way, the truth, and the life: no man cometh unto the Father, but by Me." (John 14:6)

We cannot earn salvation; we are saved by God's grace when we have faith in His Son, Jesus Christ.

Read what the Bible says, "That if thou shalt confess with thy mouth the Lord Jesus, and shalt believe in thine heart that God hath raised him from the dead, thou shalt be saved. For with the heart man believeth unto righteousness; and with the mouth confession is made unto salvation." (Rom. 10:9-10)

Please answer these questions and confess:

    a. Do you believe in your heart that Jesus Christ died on the cross for your sins?

    b. Do you believe in your heart that God raised Jesus from the dead?

    c. Would you like to receive God's forgiveness and make the decision today to turn from sin and to Christ?

4. <u>Receive Him into your life right now. THIS MOMENT!</u>

Pray this prayer:

Lord Jesus, come into my life. Forgive me of all my sins. I believe you are the Son of God and that you died on the cross for me, was buried, and then rose from the dead. Thank you for loving me enough to die for me. I accept you into my heart and give myself totally to you. Give me a new heart and a new spirit now. You are now my Savior; you are now my Lord! "I am saved!" In the name of Jesus, I pray. Amen.

Congratulations! You are now a new creature in Christ!

2 Corinthians 5:17 says,

"Therefore, if any man be in Christ, he is a new creature: old things are passed away; behold, all things are become new."

You have a whole new life with Jesus to look forward to beginning today!

Thus, the new convert can have the assurance or reaffirmed assurance of having a personal and proper relationship with and to Jesus Christ.[17] Furthermore, the new believer can commence his/her lifelong spiritual formation journey as a disciple growing into Christlikeness.[18]

CHAPTER 4

FOUNDATIONAL FACTORS RELATIVE TO GOD'S IMAGE IN MANKIND

The creation narrative is recorded in Genesis chapter 1 and culminated on the sixth day with God's declaration and work of the creation of man. Affirmatively, the Scripture states, "Then God said, 'Let us make mankind in our image, in our likeness,' … So God created mankind in his own image, in the image of God he created them; male and female he created them" (Gen. 1:26-27 NIV). Additionally, the Scripture explicates in Genesis 2:7 (NIV), "Then the Lord God formed a man from the dust of the ground and breathed into his nostrils the breath of life, and the man became a living being." Thus, in His own similitude, God made mankind to have dominion in and over all the earth realm, true righteousness, spiritual personality, nature, temperament, disposition, behavior character, moral discernment, and holiness as He does.[19] Notably, when God breathed into man the breath of life, this would be when He imparted into man his spiritual life and capacity for eternal life; his mind, thinking faculties, intellect, emotions, will, character, and personality; his ability to speak and walk; and all of the qualities that made mankind like God.[20] Thus, originally, at creation, mankind's nature and orientation were wholly toward

God.[21] G.C. Berkouwer corroborates that man was "good, righteous, holy, and capable in all things to will agreeably to the will of God."[22] Therefore, Paul's exhortation in Ephesians 5:1 for the believers to be imitators of God and the declaration in Romans 8:29 that God had predestined those He foreknew to be conformed to the image of His Son are consistent with God's initial plan for mankind to be in the likeness and image of the Godhead. Notably, the work of sanctification that Paul describes in 1 Thessalonians 5:23 is that the God of peace would perform and preserve the believer as blameless at the coming of our Lord Jesus Christ in his/her whole spirit, soul, and body, which is the state of wholesomeness in which God created mankind.[23] Subsequently, the repercussion of the fall of mankind in Genesis 3 is when God's creation of man in His image and likeness became marred. After the commission of the sin of disobedience, man undergoes a radical change in his nature and is wholly turned away from God.[24] In Genesis 2:17 (NKJV), God warns of the impending consequence of man's willful violation of the prohibition given by God and states, "for in the day that you eat of it you shall surely die." Notably, the Scriptures teach about three types of death: physical death, which entails the separation of the spirit and soul from the body, spiritual death, which entails the "separation of the individual from God," and eternal death or second death, which entails "separation from God forever which is the final state of the lost person in the lake of fire" (Rev. 20:10, 14).[25] Consequently, man's fall into sin constituted spiritual death because "man lost his communion" and intimate fellowship with God.[26] Man's spiritual death as Berkouwer explicates entailed the dying of man's "understanding that was adorned with a true and saving knowledge of his Creator, and of spiritual things."[27] Additionally, with the

Fall, the state of uprightness of man's heart and will, the purity of man's affections, and the holiness of the whole man in which mankind was originally formed and created died out.[28] Thus, a plan and process of salvation, redemption, restoration, reconciliation, and transformation of man's spiritual life were necessary. The Scripture, Genesis 3:15, states the loving Father's first prophetic pronouncement of the gospel of redemption.[29] Thus, an essential foundational factor is for the new convert and/or the young disciple to understand that God's overarching goal is for him/her to be like Him (Eph. 5:1). Subsequently, through the continuous engagement of Christian education, the believer can have the resources and support essential to the pursuit of spiritual maturity as manifested by progressive Christlikeness in his/her daily walk.

CHAPTER 5

UNDERSTANDING MANKIND AS A TRIUNE BEING: SPIRIT, SOUL, AND BODY

The Scripture in I Thessalonians 5:23 describes mankind as tripartite-spirit, soul, and body.[30] Relative to being created in the image and likeness of God, mankind is a spirit being. Mankind possesses a soul that encompasses his/her mind, will, and emotions, and mankind lives in a body.[31] How mankind formed a tripart nature was described in the previous section, "Foundational Factors Relative to God's Image in Mankind," namely, the references to Scriptures in Genesis 1:26-27 and Genesis 2:7. The enlightenment of the working knowledge of the differentiation of spirit and soul concurrent with the distinction in their functions is essential to individuals who pursue growth and development in spiritual life and maturity.[32] Subsequently, the ability to discern what is the spirit and spiritual undergirds the believer to walk according to the spirit that is consistent with the way of Jesus.[33]

Diagram one is a functional representation of mankind that employs the three circles to communicate the relationship of mankind's spirit, soul, and body.[34]

Diagram one[35]

Replicating the image of a target structure, the outer circle represents mankind's body and is the house in which he/she lives.[36] Notably, the body is the dimension of mankind that deals with the outward physical realm; thereby, it can be physically seen and touched and provides world consciousness.[37] Accordingly, the body holds the five senses: sight, smell, hearing, taste, and touch.[38] The first inward circle represents the soul, which is the inner dimension of mankind and comprises his/her mental realm.[39] Thus, being the organ of the mental realm, the soul is the component of mankind that is the intellect—it reasons and thinks.[40] Notably, the soul is the real self-life of mankind that reveals his/her personality and is the organ of self-consciousness.[41] The intricacies of mankind's soul—the mind, will, and emotions—operate in a close relationship with mankind's body.[42] Subsequently, through the soul, the body is directed "what to do, when to do it, and how to do it."[43] The second inner circle is the center, represents mankind's spirit, and is the core of his/her being.[44] Having been created in the likeness of God, mankind was designed to be governed by his spirit. The spirit is the dimension of mankind that deals with the spiritual realm and is deemed as the constituent of God-consciousness.[45] Thus, the spirit is the component or spiritual organ through which mankind communes and creates fellowship with God and is able to perceive and worship God.[46]

Consequently, with the aforementioned fall of mankind, mankind experienced spiritual death and lost the indwelling and communion of the Spirit of God within mankind's spirit. Therefore, now being spiritually dead, mankind is subject to being ruled by the dictates of what emanates from the soulish realm of his/her mind/intellect, will, and emotions. The soul touches the spirit and the body.[47] Watchman Nee elucidates that "the power of the soul is most substantial," and notably, at creation, and until the fall of mankind, the power of the soul was totally under the influence of the spirit, and the strength of the soul emanated from the spirit's strength.[48] However, because of mankind's spiritual death, the whole man was no longer controlled by the influence of the spirit through the soul, which subsequently exercised the spirit's guidance and directives to the body to obey.[49] Thus, in this fallen spiritual state, mankind primarily functions out of and is governed by the soulish realm and believes "what he/she thinks and feels is reality."[50] Diagram two represents mankind by employing three circles to illustrate the relationship of mankind's spirit, soul, and body after the fall of mankind and depicts mankind's soul as the most prominent component of the whole being.[51]

Diagram two [52]

Notably, in mankind's rebellion wherein "living in communion with God" was forfeited, and as recorded in Genesis 3:22-24, mankind was expelled from the Garden of Eden, his God-provided paradise.[53] The consequence of mankind being driven out of the Garden of Eden with a guard set to prevent mankind's reentry indicates the gravity of sin and depth of mankind's fall.[54] Berkouwer elucidates that throughout the Old Testament, God's displeasure with mankind's corruption is evident.[55] Additionally, the New Testament affirms the "radicality of sin" and its negative effects on mankind's whole being.[56] Berkouwer further delineates that Jesus' preaching "presupposes this undeniable reality of sin," whereas on one occasion, Jesus describes and addresses His listeners as evil (Matt. 7:11).[57] Thus, when Jesus is questioned regarding His dining with tax collectors and sinners, Jesus declares, "For I did not come to call the righteous, but sinners, to repentance" (Matt. 9:11-13 NKJV).[58] Hence, the commencement of the fulfillment of God's promise of His divine grace as was declared in Genesis 3:15 was manifested. The Old Testament progressively unveils the account of how by God's compassion, a remnant of Israel was preserved from the judgement and wrath of God because of Israel's continuous rebellion and disobedience to His laws and governance.[59] Similarly, the New Testament discloses how God's compassion made provisions for the ultimate sacrifice and atonement for the penalty of mankind's sins to be appeased, as is declared in John 3:16-17. Thus, Jesus affirms that the relativizing of mankind's alienation from the life of God, which in essence is the underpinning for his/her being radically sinful and evil, is not an option to reconcile or escape mankind's lost condition.[60] In the initial verses 1-7 of John chapter 3, Jesus reveals the remedy for mankind's lost, corrupt condition when He answers Nicodemus' inquiry, "…, Except a man be born again, he cannot see the kingdom of God.".... Jesus answers, "Verily, verily, I say unto thee, except a man be born of water and of the Spirit, he cannot enter into the kingdom of God. That which is born of the flesh is flesh; and that which is born of the Spirit is spirit. Marvel not that I said unto thee, Ye must be born again" (NIV). Jesus further explicates regarding the remedy to mankind's lost condition, according to John 3:15 (NKJV), "that whoever believes in Him should not perish but have eternal life." Accordingly, per the instructions in Romans 10:9-10 and Ephesians 2:8-9, when with the mouth an individual confesses unto salvation and receives by faith of the grace of God in the Lord Jesus Christ, he/she has all the benefits of the substitutionary death and resurrection of Christ. 2 Corinthians 5:17 (NKJV) describes the state of the individual who has received this benefit of new life in Christ, "Therefore, if anyone *is* in Christ, *he is* a new creation; old things have passed away; behold, all things have become new." The Scripture further teaches that this new life is from and is of God, who has reconciled us (mankind) to Himself, making peace with us through Jesus Christ and acquitting mankind of the guilt and penalty of sin (2 Cor. 5:18). Subsequently, being born of the spirit by receiving the gospel of Jesus Christ, which is the "power of God that brings salvation to everyone who believes," is the provision by which each individual can experience God's original design for mankind to have a personal relationship, walk, and fellowship with the Father and His Son Jesus Christ (Rom. 1:16 NIV; 1 John 1:23). Confirmatively, 1 Peter 1:23 (NKJV) elucidates that mankind is "born again, not of corruptible (perishable) seed, but incorruptible (imperishable) seed through the Word of God which lives and abides."

Notably, in the Scripture in 1 Peter 2:2, Apostle Peter instructs and exhorts all believers in the Christian community of faith to pursue spiritual growth and to have an avid hunger and thirst for the Word of God[61] Now, being regenerated through the experience of the new birth, the individual is as a newborn baby with the Spirit of God alive in him/her. Thus, as a believer, the individual has come into the first stage of discipleship and can progress to stage two, which entails the process of growing into Christian maturity.[62] Illustration A is a representation of mankind and employs the outline of a human figure to communicate the factor of mankind's spirit, which is as a baby at the time of his/her spiritual birth of being born again unto salvation.

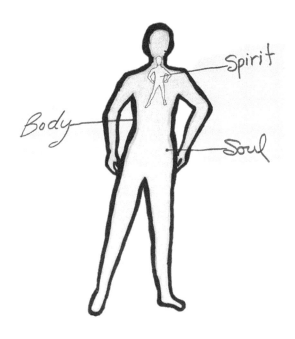

Illustration A[63]

As the believer chooses to participate and engage in Christian education through a discipleship process in a Christian community setting, he/she will have the opportunity to benefit from the spiritual ministry gifts that have been set in the Church, the body of Christ, to promote and foster continuous spiritual growth and maturity toward Christlikeness (Eph. 4:11-13). Subsequently, as the believer progresses in stage two of his/her discipleship process of Christian spiritual formation and training, the spiritual transformation of the believer is being conformed to the image His Son, Jesus Christ, as God predestined will be increasingly more manifested (Rom.8:29).[64] Thus, the believer is progressively growing into being more and more like the Son, Jesus Christ, who said in John 8:29a (NKJV), "for I always do those things that please Him." Jesus affirms that He did not seek to please Himself but to please the Father who sent Him (John 5:30; John 6:38). Additionally, Jesus exalted doing the will of God as being utmost in that He declares in John 4:34 (NKJV), "My food is to do the will of Him who sent Me, and to finish His work." The Scripture text, Romans 8:14, explicates that individuals led by the Spirit of God are sons of God. Thus, Jesus modeled walking as a blameless son being whole in His spirit, soul (mind/intellect, will, emotions), and body (1 Thess. 5:23).

Illustration B represents mankind and employs the outline of a human figure to communicate the factor of mankind's spirit having progressively developed in maturity toward attaining "the knowledge of the Son of God, toward a perfect man, and toward the measure of the stature of the fullness of Christ" (Eph. 4:13-14). Thus, spiritual growth and development encompass growing up into being steady, stable witnesses of the new life in Christ and not as wavering children (Eph. 4:13-14). The enlargement of the space that represents mankind's spirit reflects the spiritual growth that has transpired subsequent to him/her becoming a disciple of Christ who has engaged in a progressive spiritual transformation and growth process. The illustration depicts mankind's born-again spirit being in control as the locus of influence of mankind's total being, in a similar manner to how Jesus walked and in accordance with God's creation of mankind in His image and likeness.

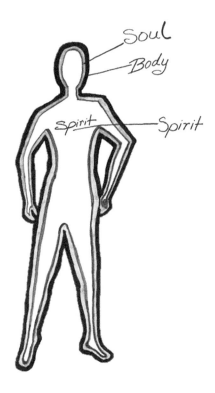

Illustration B[65]

CHAPTER 6

EIGHT ESSENTIAL ELEMENTS TO FOSTER SPIRITUAL FORMATION AND CHRISTLIKENESS

E ffective Christian education in a church setting should stimulate growth. Whether or not the believer engages in a discipleship process in a Christian community setting that uses individual one-to-one mentoring/discipling, small group engagement, study groups, spiritual coaching, or other Christian spiritual formation and training settings/forums, there are eight elements essential to spiritual growth. These elements are amenable to being inclusive in the approaches of Christian education and are foundational to the tenets of spiritual formation. The term "disciple" identifies when each believer decides to be as a follower of Jesus Christ. Additionally, the term "disciple" is the base component of Jesus' mandate to the Church, which is to make disciples. As an acrostic, the term "disciple" contains the eight essential elements that this author has determined are essential and foundational to Christian education that fosters spiritual formation and Christlikeness. The paradigm of essential elements of Christian education rendered by the outcome of this author's research work is Disciple—Dedication, Integrity,

Stewardship, Compassion, Immersion in the Word, Prayer, Learning, and Example. The Christian education paradigm delineated in this book comprises training segments designed to stimulate the growth and development of eight elements essential to spiritual formation and exhibiting Christlikeness in the believer's life.

Training Segment 1: Dedication

Bible Passages:

Luke 9:23 (AMP)[66]; Matthew 22:36-37 (NIV); John 4:34 (NKJV); Matthew 26:38-42 (NIV)

Introduction

The examination of the Scripture texts for this element reveals that Jesus explicates that the development of discipleship constitutes spiritual growth toward Christlikeness requires dedication to the level of a total commitment to following Him. By definition, the term dedication is the quality of being committed, loyal, or devoted to a task, purpose, cause, or idea.[67] Additionally, dedication can be described as the complete devotion and faith in someone or something.[68] Jesus exemplifies this element and attribute of dedication when He declares to the disciples that His completing and accomplishing the work that the Father had sent Him to do was as necessary spiritually as food is necessary physically. Subsequently, in the Garden of Gethsemane, Jesus prays the ultimate prayer of dedication. The final recorded statement of Jesus' second prayer in the Garden is "My Father, if it is not possible for this cup to be taken away unless I drink it, may your will be done" (Matt. 26:42 NIV). Hereby, Jesus expressed His total submission to finishing the work that the Father had sent Him to do as the sacrificial lamb for mankind's sin.

Expositional Application of the Spiritual Growth Element: Dedication

Per the aforementioned Scripture text and relative to the description of what dedication encompasses, an individual who makes a volitional decision to follow Jesus as His disciple must

1. Deny his/herself, which entails setting aside and forsaking all selfish interests.[69]

2. Take up his/her cross daily, expressing a willingness to endure whatever may come.

3. Follow Jesus, which entails believing in Him, conforming to His example in living, and if need be, suffering or perhaps dying because of his/her faith in Jesus.

4. Obey the commandment that is of "supreme importance and priority," which entails the individual loving the Lord God with his/her whole being—spirit, soul, and body.[70]

Symbolic Motif of Dedication:[71]

The oak tree is the selected symbolic comparative motif for the spiritual growth element and Christlike virtue of dedication. The oak tree stands tall and is sturdy. Naturally, oak wood is dependable because of its magnitude of strength, elasticity, and durability.[72] The characteristics that may be observed in the daily lifestyle of a dedicated disciple who is being spiritually formed and growing into the likeness of Christ include dependability, stability, endurance, and perseverance. The functionality and usefulness of the oak tree in the ecosystem in regard to its value to the plant and animal kingdoms are reflective of the qualities of the element of dedication. Thus, the oak tree, which is readily observable in the day-to-day environment, is a symbolic reminder and inspiration to the believer of his/her pursuit of spiritual formation and development of Christlikeness in the area of dedication as a follower of Jesus.

Training Segment 2: Integrity

Bible Passages:

Leviticus 19:11; Matthew 22:16 (NIV); Mark 12:14 (NIV); Psalm 41:12; Proverbs 10:9 (NIV); Proverbs 11:3 (NKJV)

Introduction

In the synoptic Gospels, Matthew and Mark record Jesus as having been referred to as "a man of integrity" by a select group of Pharisees and the Herodians. Although their intent was to use flattery as a means to ensnare and embolden Jesus to speak dishonorably against Rome, the element of His impeccable integrity was recognized.[73] This delegation of Jesus' opponents notes and describes that in dealing with others, Jesus is uncompromisingly truthful, honest, and impartial and that He sincerely teaches and advocates for "the way of God in accordance with the truth" (Matt. 22:16; Mark 12:14).[74] *The Strongest NIV Exhaustive Concordance* delineates the meaning of the word integrity as used in the Gospel passages referenced for this element as genuine, reliable, and trustworthy.[75] Notably, these descriptors are congruent with the character assessment of Jesus as rendered by His opponents, which were also affirmed by His savvy response to their attempted plot of ensnarement. The interpretation of the Hebrew word for integrity as used in the Old Testament is consistent with its meaning and usage in the New Testament. Particularly, the descriptors given in *The New Strong's Exhaustive Concordance of the Bible* for the Hebrew terms translated as integrity include "completeness, perfect, upright, and moral innocence."[76] Accordingly, Webster delineates the following definitions for integrity: "(1) firm adherence to a code of especially moral values; (2) incorruptibility, an unimpaired condition; (3) soundness, the quality or state of being complete or undivided; and (4) completeness."[77] Thus, in day-to-day living and in responding to life's challenges, integrity is doing what is right because it is right at all times, which encompasses when no earthly person is watching.

Expositional Application of the Spiritual Growth
Element: Integrity

Per the Scripture texts referenced above and relative to the description of what integrity encompasses, an individual who makes a volitional decision to follow Jesus as His disciple must

1. In the midst of adversity, being forsaken, and/or and challenged as per the examples of David and Jesus, to maintain uprightness, righteousness, and goodness.

2. In daily living, be uncompromising, and without rationalizing, make choices consistent with the way of God according to the counsel, wisdom, and teaching of the Scriptures.[78]

3. Hereby, electing to live morally blameless and purely, "having nothing to hide" and/or "nothing to fear."[79]

4. Live honestly and refrain from deceitful interactions and any practice of lying, which may include "distortions of the truth in word, exaggeration, actions, attitudes, or silence."[80]

Symbolic Motif of Integrity:[81]

The white lily is the selected symbolic comparative motif for the spiritual growth element and Christlike virtue of integrity. As a flower, the white lily has a broad cultural association with the qualities of beauty, purity, and modesty.[82] Notably, in "religion and art," the white lily is a symbol of purity and is commonly employed during the Easter season observance as the representative flower of the Resurrection.[83] In Scripture, as recorded in the Song of Songs 2:2, Solomon uses the lily to describe and to extol the beauty of his beloved, compared with his other daughters, and declares, "As the lily among thorns, so is my love among the daughters." [84]Additionally, in the Scripture, Jesus affirms the exceptional natural beauty of the lily in the excerpt of His discourse in Matthew 6:28-29.[85] Particularly, in Roman Catholicism, the white lily is "strongly associated with the purity of the Virgin Mary."[86] Moreover, the white lily is "commonly referred to as the Madonna Lily."[87] Thus, the white lily, which has general cultural associations in the day-to-day environment, is a symbolic reminder and inspiration to the believer of his/her pursuit of spiritual formation and development of Christlikeness in the area of integrity as a follower of Jesus.

Training Segment 3: Stewardship

Bible Passages:

Genesis 2:15; Psalm 24:1; Luke 16:1-13; Matthew 25:14-27; Luke 19:11-23; I Corinthians 12:12, 18; I Corinthians 4:1-2 (NLT)[88]; 2 Corinthians 5:18-19; I Corinthians 6:20

Introduction

Stewardship as defined by Merriam-Webster is "the conducting, supervising, or managing of something; especially the careful and responsible management of something entrusted to one's care."[89] The Learner's Dictionary concisely describes stewardship as "the activity or job of protecting and being responsible for something."[90] In accordance with the scholarly explication of the term, Charles Bugg distinctly defined Christian stewardship as "utilizing and managing all resources God provides for the glory of God and the betterment of His creation."[91] Generally, Christendom stewardship has primarily been associated with the oversight and management of money and finances.[92] However, the

Scripture provides enlightenment that as a disciple of Jesus Christ, responsible stewardship encompasses accountability to God for each aspect of his/her life.[93] The Scripture elucidates that Jesus, the chief disciple, whom the believer is following and is pursuing while growing into His likeness as our High Priest can sympathize with the believer's weaknesses because He was "in all points tempted" as each individual is but "yet without sin" (Heb. 4:15 NKJV). Jesus affirms in John 8:29b (NIV), "for I always do what pleases Him." Thus, Jesus demonstrates stalwart stewardship in the areas of life that each believer has been given the responsibility to manage and govern, including areas of spiritual life, relationships, ministry work, vocation, gifts/talents, time management, money, total health and wellness, care for the physical body, physical/temporal goods, resources, and assets.[94] Jesus expresses to the Father that he has demonstrated faithful stewardship in the ultimate task of keeping those whom the Father had given unto Him who would become the Apostles through which the ministry of the execution of the Great Commission would be commenced and would establish the Church after Jesus' ascension from the earth (Matt. 10:1-3; John 17:12).

Expositional Application of the Spiritual Growth Element: Stewardship

Per the Scripture texts referenced above and relative to the description of what stewardship encompasses, an individual who makes a volitional decision to follow Jesus as His disciple must

1. Embrace and responsibly function guided by the enlightenment that God's original plan and directive design was for mankind to be the manager and keeper of all of the resources that God placed in the earth to yield provision for him/her and all creation.

2. Embrace and responsibly function guided by the enlightenment that God is sovereign, which means that mankind is not the owner of him/herself but has been granted the privilege to use, manage, partake, enjoy, and benefit from all resources and goods available to mankind in this earth and world.

3. As a member of the body of Christ maximize the set function and work given to him/her by God as it pleases Him.

4. By the power of the Holy Spirit, be an effective witness of Christ and manager of the gospel in executing the mandate of disseminating the Word of God to the world so that all can be reconciled to God by experiencing the new birth.

Symbolic Motif of Stewardship: [95]

The coins are the selected symbolic motif for the spiritual growth element and Christlike virtue of stewardship. Money, as aforementioned, has a strong association with stewardship among the constituents of the Christian community. Moreover, in the parables referenced among the related texts for this element, Jesus uses money as a component in these teachings. Specifically, Jesus explicates that the extent of faithfulness in handling and managing wealth is an indicator of an individual's love and commitment to living and walking as a servant of God. Additionally, Paul expounds in I Timothy 6:10 (NKJV) that "for the love of money is a root of all kinds of evil, for which some have strayed from the faith in their greediness." Hence, having balance, accountability, and control in the management of money and wealth is foundational to the spiritual growth and development of faithful stewardship in all areas of the believer's life. Thus, the coins represent all the aspects of money that are used, handled, and readily observable in the day-to-day environment and serve as a symbolic reminder and inspiration to the believer of his/her pursuit of spiritual formation and development of Christlikeness in the area of stewardship as a follower of Jesus.

Training Segment 4: Compassion

Bible Passages:

Matthew 7:12; Matthew 22:39 (NIV); Matthew 18:21-33; Matthew 20:30-34; Mark 1:41; Mark 8:2-9; Luke 7:12-13; Luke 15:20; 1 Peter 3:8; 1 John 3:17

Introduction

The descriptors given in *The New Strong's Exhaustive Concordance of the Bible* for the Hebrew and Greek terms translated as "compassion" include "love, show mercy, spare, pity, mutually commiserative, feel sympathy, and to be touched with the feeling of."[96] Specifically, in regard to New Testament Greek terms translated as compassion, W. E. Vines delineates the following meanings: "to have pity, a feeling of distress through the ills of others; to be moved as to one's inwards, to be moved with compassion, to yearn with compassion; to suffer with another, to be affected similarly; to have mercy, to show kindness, by beneficence, or assistance." [97]

The definition of compassion explicated by Merriam-Webster and the aforementioned biblical scholars is unequivocally congruent. Webster's definition explicitly describes what is observed in the Scripture, which entails "sympathetic consciousness of others' distress together with a desire to alleviate it."[98] The demonstrations of compassion by God, Jesus, and others were, as Webster additionally states, "compassion implies pity coupled with an urgent desire to aid or to spare."[99]

Although compassion is a prominent virtue exemplified and observed in Old Testament Scripture, the focus of this book entails New Testament Scripture passages because the subject of this book entails fostering the examination and emulation of the way of Jesus. Notably, accounts of Jesus' compassion in Scripture include "for the multitude (Matt. 9:36; 14:14; 15:32), the unfortunate (Matt. 20:34), the leper (Mark 1:41), and the bereaved (Luke 7:13)."[100]

Expositional Application of the Spiritual Growth Element: Compassion

Per the Scripture texts referenced above and relative to the description of what compassion encompasses, an individual who makes a volitional decision to follow Jesus as His disciple must

1. In interacting, engaging, and/or responding to another and/or others, consistently be guided, governed, and influenced by what is universally known as the Golden Rule: "Do unto others as you would have them do unto you."

2. Consistently have and demonstrate feelings of care and concern for another individual to the degree of being able to show genuine empathy, seek to give aide, and help relieve the individual's suffering, need, and/or lack.

3. Maintain being loving, humble, forgiving, and merciful when interacting, engaging, and/or responding to another who is being or has been subject to evil, insulting, and/or overall impious influences or conduct.

4. Live as a vessel that the Lord can freely use as a conduit to bring blessings that pertain to life and godliness to another and/or others.

Symbolic Motif of Compassion:[101]

Hands are the selected symbolic motif for the spiritual growth element and Christlike virtue of compassion. The distinguishing factor of the exhibition of compassion is that having the feeling of sympathy, being mutually commiserative, and/or being touched with the feeling of another become a stimulus to take action to provide aid and/or relieve from distress."[102] Jesus is moved by compassion in each scriptural account and responds by initiating the use of self in a manner to relieve suffering or to fulfill the need of another and/or others. Thus, hands that are readily observable and available in day-to-day living are a symbolic reminder and inspiration to the believer of his/her pursuit of spiritual formation and development of Christlikeness in the area of compassion as a follower of Jesus.

Training Segment 5: Immersion in the Word

Bible Passages:

Joshua 1:8 (NLT); Psalm 119:8, 9, 11, 128; Proverbs 7:3; Romans 12:2; Isaiah 55:8-9 (NCV)[103]

Introduction

Immersion in the Word is an analogy for the state of an individual being completely submerged in water during a baptism.[104] Related synonyms for the term immersion include "absorption, attention, concentration, engrossment, and enthrallment."[105] Each of these synonyms can serve as a comparable descriptive term as an indicator of the intensity of this element, such as absorption, attention, concentration, engrossment, or enthrallment in the Word. Thus, the concept of immersion in the Word is the essence of what constitutes the process of and the act of the spiritual discipline of meditation as illuminated in Scripture. The descriptors given in *The New Strong's*

Exhaustive Concordance of the Bible for the Hebrew and Greek terms translated as meditate include "to murmur, to ponder, imagine, mutter, speak, study, talk, utter, converse with oneself aloud, declare, muse, to take care of, and to resolve in mind."[106] *The Strongest NIV Exhaustive Concordance* delineates the following additional meanings for the terms translated as meditate: "the act of thoughtful deliberation with the implication of speaking to oneself, tell, think, and deep in thought to consider, and think on." [107] Notably, the definition of the term meditate in Merriam-Webster includes "to engage in contemplation or reflection; to focus one's thoughts on, reflect on or ponder over; and to plan or project in the mind" and is in accordance with the aforementioned biblical explication.[108] Another term that is relevant to define and describe the meaning, process, and action of immersion in the Word or to meditate in the Word is imbue. According to Merriam-Webster, imbue means "to permeate or influence" and "implies the introduction of a quality that fills and permeates the whole being."[109] Further examination of the synonyms for imbue, which include "infuse, suffuse, ingrain, inoculate, and leaven," affirm the concept and action or process of introducing "one thing into another to affect it throughout."[110] Hence, the goal of spiritual growth is immersion in the Word or to meditate in the Word, in which imbuing the Word is practiced to the degree that it affects and influences mankind's total being—spirit, soul, and body toward Christlikeness. In Luke 4:1-13, Jesus modeled the advantage of being immersed in the Word, that is, by responding in accordance with the truth of the Word that Jesus resisted each of the temptations that Satan brought to Him. Additionally, Jesus attests that His thoughts were that of the Father's when He declares to the disciples that the words and teachings that He delivered were not His own but

His Father's, who had sent Him (John 14:10, 24). Thus, because the individual is progressively transformed by the renewing of his/her mind by meditation, subsequently, he/she will be able to think thoughts and act in ways that are increasingly more consistent with the thoughts and way of God, which is indicative of growing into Christlikeness.

Expositional Application of the Spiritual Growth Element: Immersion in the Word

Per the Scripture texts referenced for the element and relative to the description of what immersion in the Word encompasses, an individual who makes a volitional decision to follow Jesus as His disciple must meditate on the Word as instructed in the Scripture. Using the term "meditate" as an acronym, the steps of meditation for a disciple to execute to become immersed in the Word are as follows:

M = Mutter the Word. Repeatedly, speak the Word in low tones to one's self (Josh.1:8 AMP; Ps. 1:1-2 NKJV; Ps. 119:148).

E = Examine the Word. Write the Word out, study it, survey it, and check out the meaning of each Word in the Scripture passage (Ps. 119:30; 105; 2 Tim. 2:15).

D = Decide to follow the Word. Determine to obey the Word, to do it (Ps. 119:105; I Tim. 4:15-16).

I = Imagine the Word visually. Create a visual image. See yourself having it, possessing it, it becoming a reality (Ps. 119:23; Eph. 3:20).

T = Think on the Word repeatedly (Phil. 4:8; Ps. 119:78).

A = Affirm the Word by studying the Scripture (2 Tim. 2:15).

T = Talk the Word aloud to one's self (Ps. 77:12; 119:15).

E = Exclaim the Word with excitement and expectancy (Ps. 119:111; Luke 1:46-47).

Symbolic Motif of Immersion in the Word:[111]

The Holy Bible is the selected symbolic motif for the spiritual growth element and Christlike virtue of immersion in the Word.

The Holy Bible is the book of books and comprises of both the Old and New Testaments. It contains the inspired inerrant Word of God, which is known as the sacred Scriptures that formulate the constitution and all that pertains to the Christian faith. Thus, the Bible as an essential element of the Christian faith is readily observable, available in day-to-day living, and is a symbolic reminder and inspiration to the believer of his/her pursuit of spiritual formation and development of Christlikeness in the area of immersion in the Word.

Training Segment 6: Prayer

Bible Passages:

Matthew 6:5-13; 7:7; 14:23; Mark 1:35; 6:46; 14:36; Luke 3:21; 5:16; 6:12; 9:18, 28; Luke 11:1-4

Introduction

In Christendom, prayer is generally defined as talking to or communicating with God. As William Mounce explicates, congruent to the Hebrew and Greek words from its translation to English, the term prayer is a noun.[112] Accordingly, the term prayer corresponds to the Hebrew and Greek words translated as the term pray, which is a verb.[113] Prayer may entail engaging in "prayer as a regular habit or as a single act."[114] Through the redemptive work of Jesus, mankind has been reconciled to God and has been restored with the ability and access to have regular communion and fellowship with God, such as the Scripture indicates that Adam did before the Fall. The believer's quality and development of spiritual life is relative to the quality of his/

her engagement in prayer. As the quality and frequency of communication are key foundational factors for establishing and building natural relationships, so it is with mankind and God. Consequently, an individual's degree of intimacy with God is predicated upon his/her level of engagement with God through the act of prayer. Subsequently, to experience spiritual formation and to grow into Christlikeness, the believer must progressively develop the spiritual discipline of prayer.[115] Accordingly, Dave Earley argues that "prayer must be prioritized and practiced to achieve maximum impact."[116] The Scripture for this element affirm through the recorded instructions as spoken by Jesus in the Gospels and as recorded in the Epistles that it is an unequivocal expectation of God and reiterated by Jesus that prayer is to be a continuous lifestyle component of the believer's walk as a Christian disciple who has a personal relationship with the Lord.[117] Notably, individuals generally, naturally, and continuously engage in conversation and/or communication with others by using the four types of sentence structures: declarative, imperative, interrogative, and/or exclamatory. Comparatively, believers generally, naturally, and continuously engage in conversation and/or communication with God that uses prayer structures such as adoration, confession, thanksgiving, and/or supplication.[118] Jesus' lifestyle manner of His prayer relationship with the Father was conspicuous. Jesus models and exhibits that his personal, consistent interaction with God, His Father, is an indispensable contingency to the effectiveness of His public ministry.[119] In Scripture, Jesus engages in and exhibits prayer as a consistent practice and often as a single act.

Expositional Application of the Spiritual Growth
Element: Prayer

Per the Scripture texts referenced for this element and relative to the description of what prayer encompasses, an individual who makes a volitional decision to follow Jesus as His
disciple must

1. Devote his/herself to prayer and make it a daily priority
   (Col. 4:2 NIV).[120]

2. Pray without ceasing, which is indicative of a continuous relationship and interaction with the Father (Eph.
   6:18; 1 Thess. 5:17).[121]

3. Use the granted privilege to approach God's throne of
   grace with confidence so that he/she may receive mercy
   and find grace to help in his/her time of need (Heb.
   4:16 NIV).

4. Recognize and celebrate positive emotions and experiences by praying prayers of adoration and/or thanksgiving (Luke 1:46-49).

5. Recognize, control, and manage negative emotions and
   experiences by using prayers of supplication, interces-
   sion, and thanksgiving. The action steps to help the
   believer to be disciplined in regulating his/her emotions
   are explained by this acronym: P-R-A-Y.

P – a. Pause, which means to stop what you are doing (Jas. 1:19 NIV)

   b. Petition—talk to the Lord, tell Him all about it (Phil. 4:6 AMP)

R – a. Reposition yourself, which might entail

   b. Removing yourself from the situation

   c. Reviewing the situation to determine who, what, how, and so forth (1 Cor. 10:13 NIV)

A – a. Assess and analyze based on the factors determined in your review of the situation

   b. Agree with the Word as it pertains to the situation

   c. Act on the Word (John 8:29 AMP; John 14:15 NIV; Isa. 1:19 NIV)

Y – a. Yield to the power of the Holy Spirit to allow Him to produce the fruit of His character in you (John 16:13 NIV; 2 Cor. 6:6 NIV).

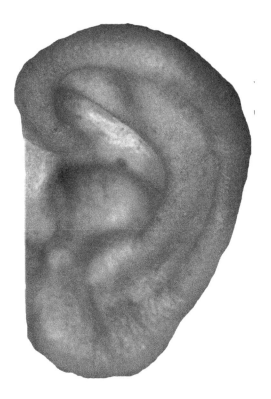

Symbolic Motif of Prayer:[122]

The ear is the selected symbolic motif for the spiritual growth element and Christlike virtue of prayer. Universally and characteristically, the ear is the organ of hearing. Thus, because the ears are used for hearing and listening in communication among and with other individuals, God affirms that He also is attentive with His ears in communication directed to Him from the believer through his/her prayers (Jas. 5:4 NIV; 1 Pet. 3:12 NIV). The Message Bible translation of Psalm 34:15 corroborates the factor of God's attentiveness to the prayers rendered by the righteous and describes them as God's friends by stating, "God keeps an eye on His friends; His ears pick up every moan and groan." This Message Bible translation also affirms that God hears the audible and inaudible prayers of the believer as he/she strives with every effort to be unceasing and persistent in prayer by continually maintaining an attitude of prayer that is not always audible. Thus, the ear, which is readily observable and used in the day-to-day living, is a symbolic reminder and inspiration to the believer of his/her pursuit of spiritual formation and development of Christlikeness in the area of prayer as a follower of Jesus.

Training Segment 7: Learning

Bible Passages:

Luke 2:52 (NIV); Matthew 7:28-29 (MSG)[123]; 2 Timothy 3:7 (NIV); Colossians 1:6-7 (NIV)

Introduction

The definition of learning in Merriam-Webster includes "the act or experience of one that learns; knowledge or skill acquired by instruction or study; and/or modification of a behavioral tendency by experience."[124] Strong explicates that the Hebrew term translated as learning means "something received mentally, instruction whether on the part of a teacher or hearer."[125] The *Strongest NIV Exhaustive Concordance*, also based on the root Hebrew and Greek terms translated, describes learning as "wisdom, skill, learning that can refer to skill in life, ability, wise advice, be instructed, and learn to get into the habit of being."[126] Notably, William Mounce corroborates and enhances the exposition of the New Testament term for learning as it relates to spiritual growth and development. Mounce affirms that "learning is an important aspect of discipleship" when he explicates that the word "disciple" is derived from the Greek verb for learning.[127] Thus, Mounce elucidates that "learning in the New Testament frequently focuses on the gospel and the teachings of the apostles."[128] Additionally, learning as it pertains to maturing and developing as a disciple of Christ encompasses the exposure, acquisition, comprehension, obedience to, and execution of truths that have been learned.[129]

Expositional Application of the Spiritual Growth Element: Learning

Per the Scripture texts referenced above and relative to the description of what learning encompasses, an individual who makes a volitional decision to follow Jesus as His disciple must

1. Engage in a process to receive instruction in the Word of God (Isa. 54:13 NIV; John 6:45 NIV).

2. Pursue the comprehension and discernment of truth (Prov. 1:2-6; 4:5-7 NIV; 2 Tim. 2:15).

3. Progressively become a doer of the Word and not a hearer only (Jas. 1:22; 1 John 2:17; Rev. 22:14 NKJV).

4. Be diligent to present him/herself as a vessel of honor, approved by God, as an effective witness and ambassador for Christ in the ministry of reconciliation (2 Tim. 2:15; 19-21; 2 Cor. 5:18, 20; Acts 1:8 NIV).

Symbolic Motif of Learning:[130]

Books pertaining to Christian topics are the selected symbolic motif for the spiritual growth element and Christlike virtue of learning. In addition to the Bible, Christian-related books and other visual or audio materials are common components of personal, small group, and/or corporate devotional time, study, teaching, training, or mentoring in spiritual growth and development endeavors. Thus, Christian-related books and materials, which are readily observable and available in the day-to-day living environment, are a symbolic reminder and inspiration to the believer of his/her pursuit of spiritual formation and development of Christlikeness in the area of learning as a follower of Jesus.

Training Segment 8: Example

Bible Passages:

Eph. 5:1-2 (NIV); John 13:14-15; John 13:34 (NIV); 2 Thess. 3:9 (NKJV); 2 Thess. 3:9 (NIV); 1 Thess. 1:7 (NKJV); 1 Pet. 5:3 (NIV); Titus 2:7 (NIV)

Introduction

The definition of the term example in Merriam-Webster is "one that serves as a pattern to be imitated; someone or something set before one for guidance or imitation."[131] The Greek terms according to Strong that are translated as example include the following definitions: "exhibit for imitation; pattern; form; a model for imitation; and copy for imitation."[132] The *Strongest NIV Exhaustive Concordance* and Mounce corroborate the aforementioned definitions because these sources define the Greek terms translated as example as a "pattern, example, model, use as a model, imitate, follow example, and a pattern of behavior to be emulated."[133] Because mankind was restored through the redemptive work of Jesus Christ in His relationship as a son of God who was created in His image, mankind has the directive to copy and follow God's example, as a dearly loved child imitates his/her father (Eph. 5:1). Additionally, the Scripture admonishes the believer to "walk in the way of love, just as Christ loved" all mankind and gave Himself for each one (Eph. 5:2). Jesus affirms that He was providing an example of humility and servanthood that should be emulated by His disciples when He engaged in washing the feet of His disciples (John 13:14-15). Also in this segment of teaching and demonstration is that Jesus presented the disciples with the new commandment, which set the foundation for becoming examples of the way of Jesus, he expounded, "A new command I give you: Love one another. As I have loved you, so you must love one another" (John 13:34).

Expositional Application of the Spiritual Growth
Element: Example

Per the Scripture texts referenced for this element and relative to the description of what example encompasses, an individual who makes a volitional decision to follow Jesus as His disciple must offer his/herself to live as an example, providing a pattern and being a concrete model to demonstrate how God wants His sons and daughters to live (Phil. 3:17 NIV).[134] In accordance with the instructions delineated by the Apostle Paul to young Timothy in 1 Timothy 4:12, the disciple of Christ should to an example for other believers in the following:

1. Speech

2. Conduct

3. Love

4. Spirit

5. Faith

6. Purity

Symbolic Motif of Example:[135]

Footsteps are the selected symbolic motif for the spiritual growth element and Christlike virtue of example. The Amplified Bible translation of the Scripture text in 1 Peter 2:21 reiterates that as a believer, he/she has been called for the purpose of following in the footsteps of Jesus who is a concrete example of how to please the Father in all that he/she does. Thus, the believer's footsteps and pattern of life, which are readily observable in his/her day-to-day living environment, are a symbolic reminder and inspiration to the believer of his/her pursuit of spiritual formation and development of Christlikeness in the area of being an example for others to follow.

CHAPTER 7

CONCLUSION

Notably, the paradigm for ministry application delineated in this book is pragmatic and adaptable to personal enhancement, a broad range of church and/or Christian communities relative to their distinctive culture and character. Furthermore, the paradigm conveys the simplicity and complexities of the gospel and kingdom principles in such a manner that fosters the perception, comprehension, and operationalization of the essential factors and elements that pertain to the pursuit of spiritual formation and Christlikeness.

In closing, considering the content of this book and the Scripture text in Romans 8:29, which provides the enlightenment that God's overarching goal for the followers of Christ is to become like Him, this author is reminded of Jesus' declaration in Luke 22:27 (NIV), "For who is greater, the one who is at the table or the one who serves? Is it not the one who is at the table? But I am among you as one who serves." Hereby, Jesus taught and modeled that the essence of greatness and His true, basic nature is that of a servant who renders His life for the sake of others. Thus, as a believer in the pursuit of Christlikeness and becoming spiritually formed into His greatest image as servant, this author offers this prayer:

"A Servant's Prayer"

Father, I am your servant and my prayer is

S – **Sanctify me**

Sanctify me and cleanse me with the washing of your word and give to me the Spirit of wisdom and revelation of Jesus Christ.

Eph. 5:26 | Eph. 1:17

E – *to* **Esteem others**

Help me to esteem others as better than myself and to do all things with humbleness of mind and without pride and selfishness.

Phil. 2:3 | Matt. 22:39

R – *to be a* **Righteous, Ready, Responsive Representative**

Fill me with the fruit of righteousness walking as His representative ready and responsive to obey His commands.

Col. 1:10 | 2 Cor.5:20 | John 4:34 | John 8:29

V – *to be* **Vigilant**

To be vigilant, sober minded and cautious at all times because my enemy, the devil, roars like a lion seeking to seize and to devour me and giving thanks to God who always leads me into triumph in Christ Jesus.

1 Pet. 5:7 | 1 Pet. 2:14 | 2 Cor. 2:14 | Jer. 29:11

A – *to* **Attend His Word**

To pay attention to God's word and to listen closely to what He says.

Prov. 4:20 | Heb. 2:1 | Isa. 1:19

N – **not my will**

Nevertheless, not my will, but yours, be done.

Luke 22:42 | John 14:15 | Jas. 1:12 | Matt. 24:13

T – *to be* **Transformed**

To be transformed by the renewing of my mind so that I can prove what is the good, acceptable and perfect will of God and be a light in the world and to function as salt in the earth.

Rom.12:2 | Matt. 5:13-14 | Phil. 2:5 | Eph. 4:23

Now, Father, I thank you for these virtues being manifested in my life. In Jesus' name, I pray…

Amen

Endnotes

NOTES

Chapter 1: Introduction

[1] Ronald T. Habermas, Introduction to Christian Education and Formation: A Lifelong Plan for Christ-Centered Restoration (Grand Rapids: Zondervan, 2008), 11.

Chapter 2: Christian Education: An Essential Process

[2] Robert E. Clark, Lin Johnson, and Allyn K. Sloat, eds., Christian Education: Foundations for the Future (Chicago: Moody Press, 1991), 21.

[3] Ibid.

[4] Ibid., 93.

[5] Eleanor Daniel, John W. Wade, and Charles Gresham, Introduction to Christian Education (Cincinnati: The Standard Publishing Company, 1993), 93.

[6] Jack L. Seymour, Teaching the Way of Jesus: Educating Christians for Faithful Living (Nashville: Abingdon Press, 1990), 38 and 65.

[7] Ibid., 65.

[8] Ibid., 72.

Chapter 3: Foundational Factors Relative to Spiritual Life

9   Dave Earley and Rod Dempsey, Disciple Making Is...:
    How to Live the Great Commission with Passion and
    Confidence (Nashville, TN: B&H Publishing, 2013), 19.

10 Note: NKJV is the abbreviation for the New King James
    Version.

11 Clark, Johnson, and Sloat, Christian Education, 21;
    Ronald T. Habermas, The Complete Disciple: A Model
    for Cultivating God's Image in Us (Colorado Springs:
    Cook Communications Ministries, 2003), 13.

12 Charles E. Lewis, Possessing the Keys of the Ministries
    New Member's Book (Durham: LL&L Printing & Design
    Company, 2014), 6.

13 Ibid.

14 Ibid.

15 Ibid.

16 Ibid.

17 Walter A. Hendrichsen. Disciples Are Made Not Born:
    Helping Others Grow to Maturity in Christ (Colorado
    Springs: David C. Cook, 1998), 59.

18 Ibid.

Chapter 4: Foundational Factors Relative to God's Image
             in Mankind

19 King James Study Bible, 7; G.C. Berkouwer, Studies in
    Dogmatics Man: The Image of God (Grand Rapids: Wm.
    B. Eerdmans Publishing Company, 1984), 38–39.

20 Ibid., 7–8; Habermas, The Complete Disciple, 26.

21 Berkouwer, Studies in Dogmatics Man, 38.

22 Ibid.

23 Habermas, The Complete Disciple, 27.

24 Berkouwer, Studies in Dogmatics Man, 38.

25 King James Study Bible, 10.

26 Berkouwer, Studies in Dogmatics Man, 38.

27 Ibid., 39.

28 Ibid.

29 King James Study Bible, 13–14.

Chapter 5: Understanding Mankind as a Triune Being: Spirit, Soul, and Body

30 Watchman Nee, The Spiritual Man, Vol. 1 (New York: Christian Fellowship Publishers, Inc., 1969), 21; Ray S. Anderson, On Being Human Essays in Theological Anthropology (Eugene: Wipf and Stock Publishers, 1991), 207–214.

31 Nee, The Spiritual Man, 35–38.

32 Ibid, 11.

33 Ibid.

34 Andrew Wommack, Spirit, Soul and Body Study Guide (Colorado Springs, CO: Wommack Ministries, Inc., 2008), 24.

35 This graphic depicts the three-fold nature of mankind before the Fall of mankind. It illustrates that mankind's spirit operated as the most prominent component of mankind's total being before the Fall. Designed by and used

by permission of Shawntae L. McKnight, LL&L Printing
& Design Company.

36 Wommack, Spirit, Soul and Body Study Guide, 19.

37 Nee, The Spiritual Man, 26; Wommack, Spirit, Soul and
    Body Study Guide, 19.

38 Lester Sumrall, Spirit, Soul & Body: Bring Wholeness
    and Joy Into Your Life (New Kensington: Whitaker
    House, 1995), 55.

39 Wommack, Spirit, Soul and Body Study Guide, 19.

40 Nee, The Spiritual Man, 35–40.

41 Ibid., 26; Sumrall, Spirit, Soul & Body, 35.

42 Sumrall, Spirit, Soul & Body, 35.

43 Ibid.

44 Wommack, Spirit, Soul and Body Study Guide, 19–20.

45 Nee, The Spiritual Man, 26.

46 Ibid.

47 Ibid., 27; Wommack, 20.

48 Nee, The Spiritual Man, 27.

49 Ibid.

50 Wommack, Spirit, Soul and Body Study Guide, 20.

51 Ibid., 24.

52 This graphic depicts the three-fold nature of mankind
    after the Fall of mankind. It illustrates that the soul oper-
    ates as the most prominent component of mankind's total
    being after the Fall. Designed by and used by permission

of Shawntae L. McKnight, LL&L Printing & Design Company.

[53] Berkouwer, Studies in Dogmatics Man, 142.

[54] Ibid.

[55] Ibid.

[56] Ibid.

[57] Ibid.

[58] Ibid.

[59] Ibid.

[60] Ibid.

[61] Michael Rydelink and Michael Vanlaningham, eds., The Moody Bible Commentary (Chicago: Moody Publishers, 2014), 1960.

[62] Earley and Dempsey, Disciple Making Is, 128–129.

[63] This drawing is used by permission from Wilbert J. O'Neal.

[64] Earley and Dempsey, Disciple Making Is, 126–129.

[65] This drawing is used by permission from Wilbert J. O'Neal.

Chapter 6: Eight Essential Elements to Foster Spiritual Formation and Christlikeness

[66] Note: AMP as used in this book is the abbreviation for the Amplified Bible.

67 Merriam-Webster Dictionary, s.v. "dedication," accessed January 28, 2020, https://www.merriam-webster.com/dictionary/dedication.

68 Ibid.

69 Earley and Dempsey, Disciple Making Is, 86.

70 King James Study Bible, 1467.

71 Oak Tree photograph was taken and used by permission of Brandi K. Autry Photography & Design.

72 Encycopedia.com, s.v. "oak," accessed November 14, 2019, https://www.encyclopedia.com/plants-and-animals/plants/plants/oak.

73 Rydelink and Vanlaningham, The Moody Bible Commentary, 1494 and 1539.

74 Ibid., 1539.

75 Edward W. Goodrick and John R. Kohlenberger III, The Strongest NIV Exhaustive Concordance (Grand Rapids: Zondervan, 2004), 239.

76 James Strong, The New Strong's Exhaustive Concordance of the Bible (Nashville: Thomas Nelson Publishers, 1990), 8537.

77 Merriam-Webster Dictionary, s.v. "integrity," accessed January 28, 2020, https://www.merriam-webster.com//integrity.

78 Chuck Broughton, The Character of a Follower of Jesus Design for Discipleship 4 (Colorado Springs: NavPress, 2006), 61.

79 Rydelink and Vanlaningham, The Moody Bible Commentary, 912.

80 Broughton, The Character of a Follower of Jesus Design for Discipleship 4, 71.

81 White Lily photograph was taken and used by permission of Lucrecia A. High.

82 Andrea Howland-Myers, "What Is the Meaning of White Lilly?" accessed November 15, 2019, https://www.hunker.com/12350961/what-is-the-meaning-of-white-lilly.

83 The Columbia Encyclopedia, 6th ed., s.v. "lily," accessed November 29, 2019, Encyclopedia.com, https://www.encyclopedia.com/reference/encyclopedias-almanacs-transcripts-and-maps/lily.

84 Ibid.; Rydelink and Vanlaningham, The Moody Bible Commentary, 993.

85 The Columbia Encyclopedia, "lily."

86 Ibid.

87 Ibid.

88 Note: NLT is the abbreviation for New Living Translation.

89 Merriam-Webster Dictionary, s.v. "stewardship," accessed December 1, 2019, https://www.merriam-webster.com/dictionary/stewardship.

90 Learner's Dictionary, s.v. "stewardship," accessed December 1, 2019, http://www.learnersdictionary.com/definition/stewardship.

91 Ibid.

92 Ibid.

93 Chuck Broughton, Growing in Discipleship Design for Discipleship 6 (Colorado Springs: NavPress, 2006), 25.

94 Ibid.

95 Coins photograph was taken and used by permission of Lucrecia A. High.

96 Strong, The New Strong's Exhaustive Concordance of the Bible, 7355, 2560, 7349, 4697, 4835, 2550, and 7356.

97 W.E. Vine, Merrill F. Unger, and William White, Vine's Complete Expository Dictionary of W.E. Old and New Testament Words (Nashville: Thomas Nelson, Inc., 1985), 116.

98 Merriam-Webster Dictionary, s.v. "compassion," accessed December 6, 2019, https://www.merriam-webster.com/dictionary/compassion.

99 Ibid.

100 Frank C. Thompson, "Compassion," Thompson Chain Reference (1908), accessed December 6, 2019, https://www.studylight.org/concordances/tcr/c/compassion.html.

101 Hands photograph was taken and used by permission of Lucrecia A. High.

102 Strong, The New Strong's Exhaustive Concordance of the Bible, 7355, 2560, 7349, 4697, 4835, 2550, and 7356.

103 Note: NCV as used in this book is the abbreviation for the New Century Version.

104 Merriam-Webster Dictionary, s.v. "immersion," accessed December 8, 2019, https://www.merriam-webster.com/dictionary/immersion.

105 Ibid.

106   Strong, The New Strong's Exhaustive Concordance of the Bible, 7878, 1897, and 3191.

107   Goodrick and Kohlenberger, The Strongest NIV Exhaustive Concordance, 2047 and 8488.

108   Merriam-Webster Dictionary, s.v. "meditate," accessed December 8, 2019, https://www.merriam-webster.com/dictionary/meditate.

109   Merriam-Webster Dictionary, s.v. "imbue," accessed December 8, 2019, https://www.merriam-webster.com/dictionary/imbue.

110   Ibid.

111   Bible photograph was taken and used by permission of Lucrecia A. High.

112   William D. Mounce, ed., Mounce's Complete Expository Dictionary of Old & New Testament Words (Grand Rapids: Zondervan, 2006), 532.

113   Ibid.

114   Ibid.

115   Donald S. Whitney, Spiritual Disciplines for the Christian Life (Colorado Springs: Navpress, 1991), 66 and 69.

116   Dave Earley, Prayer: The Timeless Secret of High-Impact Leaders (Chattanooga: Living Ink Books, 2008), x.

117   Whitney, Spiritual Disciplines for the Christian Life, 67.

118   Earley, Prayer, 129–130.

119   Mark Jones, The Prayers of Jesus: Listening to and Learning from Our Savior (Wheaton: Crossway, 2019), 46.

[120] Whitney, Spiritual Disciplines for the Christian Life, 67.

[121] Ibid.

[122] Ear photograph was taken and used by permission of Lucrecia A. High.

[123] Note: MSG as used in this book is the abbreviation for The Message.

[124] Merriam-Webster Dictionary, s.v. "learning," accessed January 1, 2020, https://www.merriam-webster.com/dictionary/learning.

[125] Strong, The New Strong's Exhaustive Concordance of the Bible, 3948.

[126] Goodrick and Kohlenberger, The Strongest NIV Exhaustive Concordance, 2683 and 3443.

[127] Mounce, Mounce's Complete Expository Dictionary of Old & New Testament Words, 397.

[128] Ibid.

[129] Ibid.

[130] Christian Books photograph was taken and used by permission of Lucrecia A. High.

[131] Merriam-Webster Dictionary, s.v. "example," accessed January 5, 2020, https://www.merriam-webster.com/dictionary/example#synonym-discussion.

[132] Strong, The New Strong's Exhaustive Concordance of the Bible, 5262, 5179, and 5261.

[133] Mounce, Mounce's Complete Expository Dictionary of Old & New Testament Words, 226; Goodrick

and Kohlenberger, The Strongest NIV Exhaustive Concordance, 5682, 3629, 5213, 3628, 5596, and 5681.

134 Mounce, Mounce's Complete Expository Dictionary of Old & New Testament Words, 226.

135 Footsteps photograph was taken and used by permission of Lucrecia A. High.

Lightning Source UK Ltd.
Milton Keynes UK
UKHW051829300123
416190UK00001B/12